Animal Look-Alikes

By Rachel Griffiths and Margaret Clyne

Contents

Introduction

Some animals look alike. Different animals are never exactly the same, though. This book will help you learn to tell the differences between some animals that look alike.

Butterflies and Moths

Butterflies and moths are alike in some ways. They are both **insects**. Both have wings and antennae. Both usually feed on plant nectar.

Life Cycle of a Butterfly or a Moth

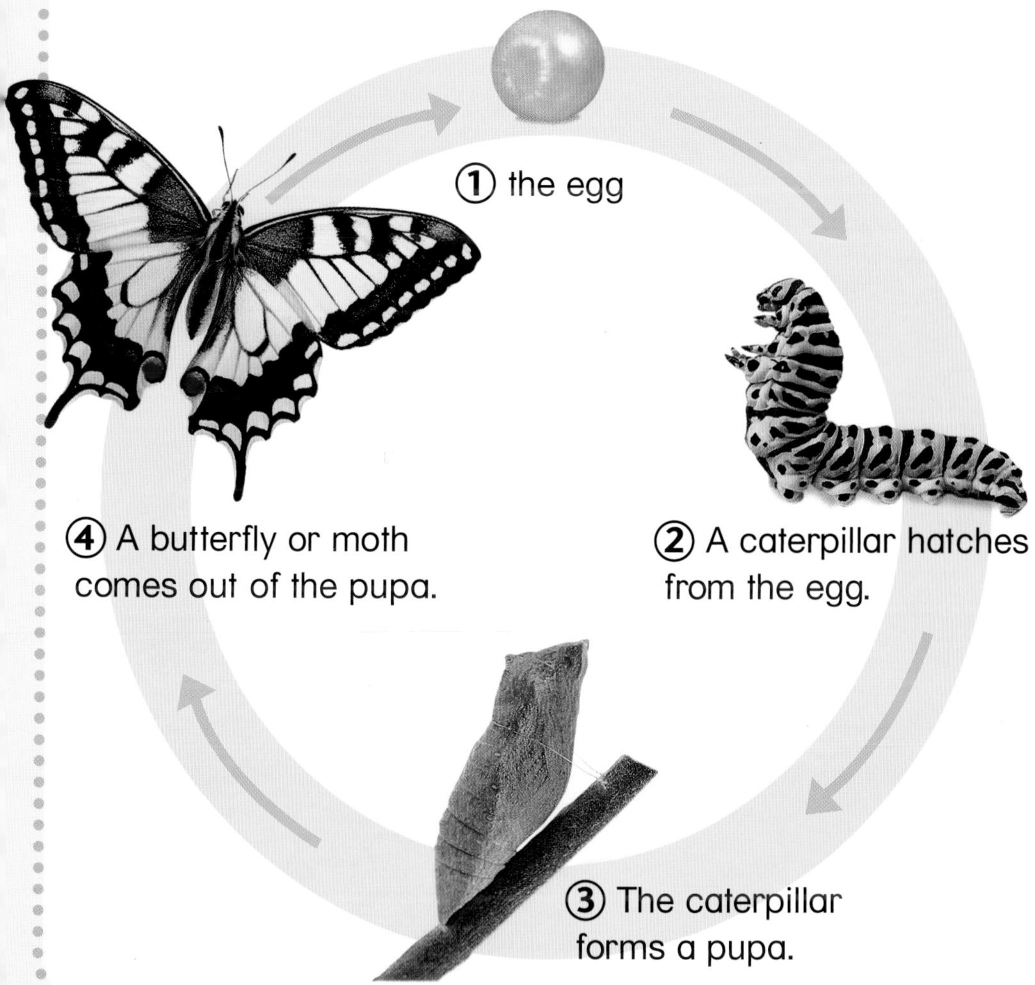

Butterflies and moths also have similar **life cycles**. They both lay eggs and spend part of their lives as caterpillars. Are butterflies and moths exactly alike?

Butterflies and moths are not the same. Most moths have wide, furry bodies. Butterflies have thinner bodies that are not furry.

Butterflies have knobs on the ends of their antennae. Moths do not. Many moth antennae look like feathers.

◀ **puss moth**

▲ **comma butterfly**

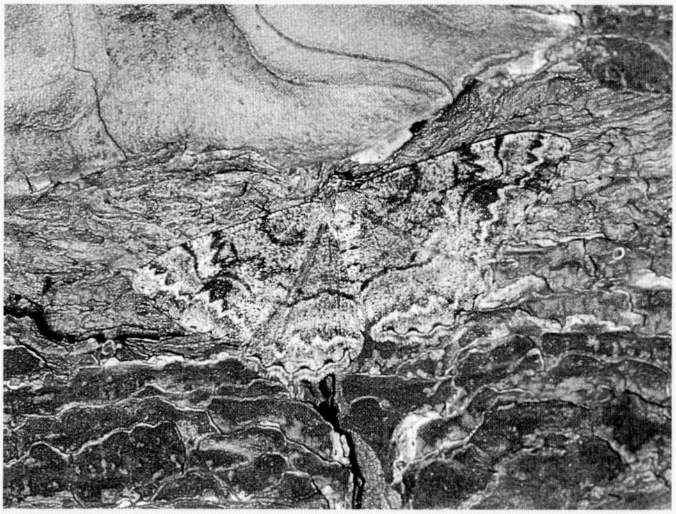

It is hard to see this moth because it is almost the same colour as the tree bark.

▲ **acacia carpenter moth**

▲ **Cleopatra butterfly**

Butterflies are usually more colourful than moths. Moths are often brown or grey. These dull colours help moths hide. This is called **camouflage**.

Alligators and Crocodiles

Alligators and crocodiles are alike in some ways. They are both **reptiles**. They both have bumpy skin, short legs and long, strong tails.

Alligators and crocodiles are both good swimmers. They both have very sharp teeth, and both will eat any kind of animal they can catch. Are alligators and crocodiles exactly alike?

Alligators and crocodiles are not the same. Alligators have rounded snouts. Crocodile snouts are more pointed.

Alligators and crocodiles have different jaws, too. When an alligator closes its mouth, most of its teeth are hidden. Crocodile teeth stick out of their closed mouths. They make it look like the crocodile is smiling.

Is it an alligator or a crocodile?

Places Where Alligators and Crocodiles Live

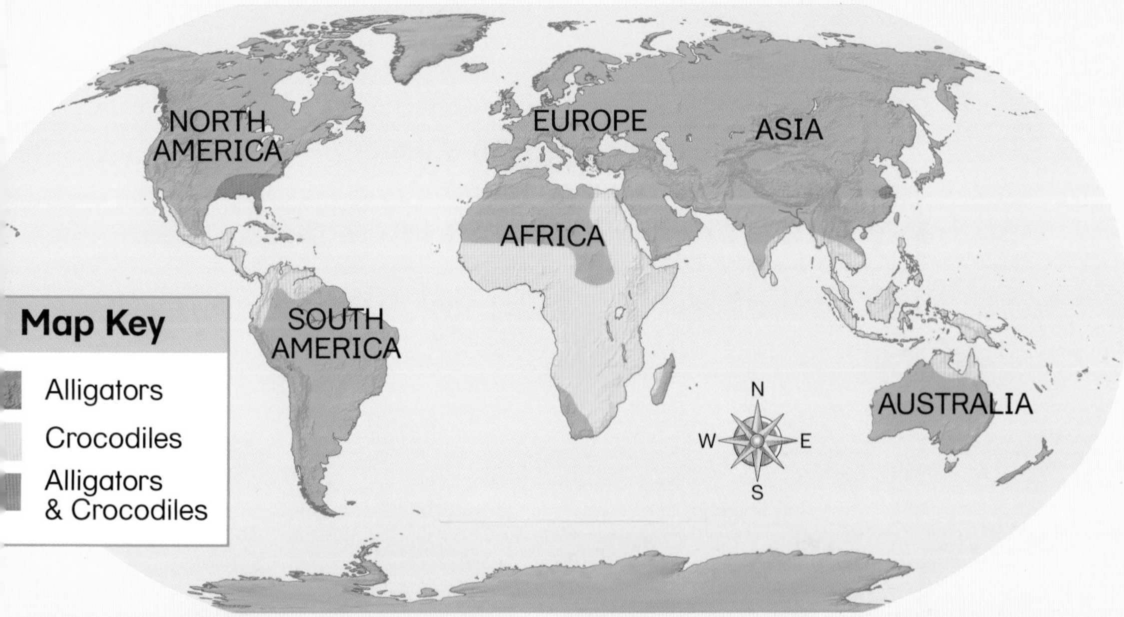

Many North American alligators live in Florida.

Crocodiles live in the Northern Territory of Australia.

Alligators and crocodiles are found around the world. Alligators live only in the United States and China. Crocodiles live in North America and Asia, and in South America, Africa and Australia.

Frogs and Toads

Frogs and toads are alike in some ways. They are both **amphibians**. They both have four legs and can have green or brown skin. They both have eyes that stick out, and both eat insects.

Life Cycle of a Frog or a Toad

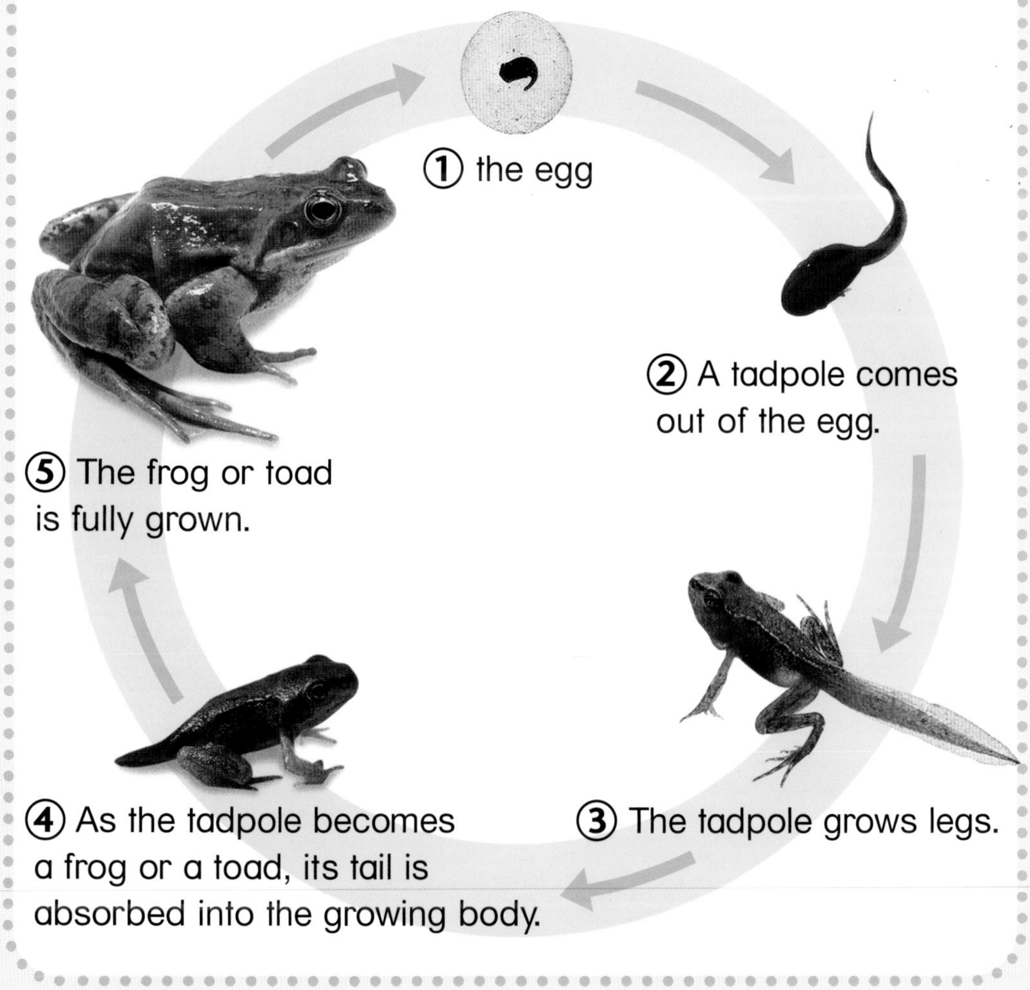

Frogs and toads also have similar life cycles. They both start out as eggs. Then they hatch into tadpoles and live under water. Finally, they become adults and hop onto land. Are frogs and toads exactly alike?

Frogs and toads are not the same. Frogs have smooth and wet skin. Toads have bumpy and dry skin. Toads usually have wider bodies than frogs, too.

Frogs and toads usually live in different **environments**. Many frogs spend a lot of time in or near the water. Toads live mostly on land.

Seals and Sea Lions

Seals and sea lions are alike in some ways. They are both **mammals**. Both have sleek fur and flippers that they use to move quickly in water.

▲ seals

Sea lions and seals live in the ocean. They are great swimmers and divers. Both catch their food as they swim.

Sea lions and seals both climb onto land to rest and to have their babies. Are sea lions and seals exactly alike?

sea lions ▼

Sea lions and seals are not the same. Sea lions are bigger than seals. They are also noisier. They make loud barking sounds, but seals make softer, grunting sounds.

Both animals hear well. However, seals have tiny ear holes, while sea lions have ear flaps on the sides of their heads.

▼ sea lion

Seals and sea lions move on land in different ways. Sea lions pull their hind flippers forward and move using all four flippers. Seals move along on their stomachs.

A seal moves on its stomach.

A sea lion holds its body up when it uses its flippers to move.

Look-alikes Everywhere

Animal look-alikes come in all shapes and sizes. Some are insects, some are mammals, some are reptiles and some are amphibians.

Up close animal look-alikes can be quite different. These differences make each animal unique.

▲ leopard

▲ cheetah

Other Animal Look-alikes

rabbit

hare

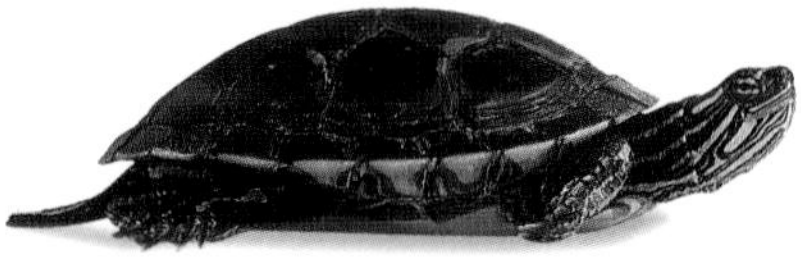
turtle

tortoise

hedgehog

echidna

coyote

wolf

Further Reading

Learn more about animal look-alikes by reading the books listed below.

Books:

Animal Encyclopedia
by Chris Packham
Dorling Kindersley, 2000

Eye Wonder Mammals
Dorling Kindersley, 2002

Learn more about animal look-alikes by visiting the websites listed below.

Websites:

National Geographic Kids site:
www.nationalgeographic.com/kids

Natural History Museum:
www.nhm.ac.uk

Kids Planet site:
www.kidsplanet.org

Glossary

amphibians	types of animals that can live on land and in water
camouflage	the colour or shape of an animal that helps it hide
environments	the conditions in an area including the variety of living things, the type of land and the climate
insects	types of animals that have three body parts and six legs
life cycles	all the changes animals or plants go through as they grow
mammals	animals that are fed with their mother's milk; mammals have fur or hair
reptiles	types of coldblooded animals that often have scales and lay eggs

Index